A CENTURY of
THE BLACK COUNTRY

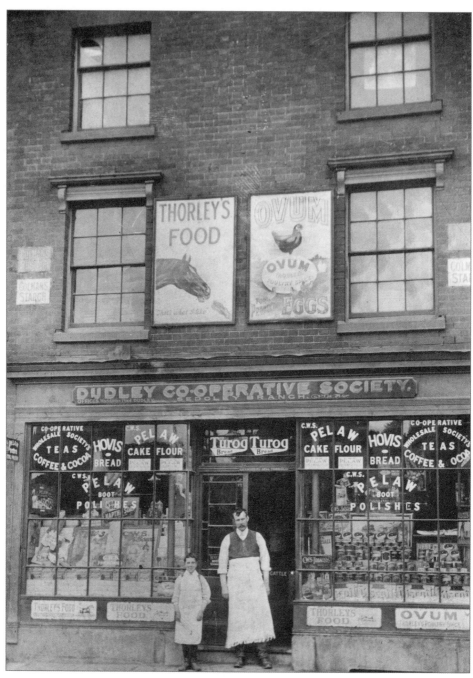

The Sedgley branch of the Dudley Co-operative Society, *c.* 1910. In the doorway stands the manager, Simeon Turner and young Ben Flavell. (*T. Burford Collection*)

A CENTURY of
THE BLACK COUNTRY

NED WILLIAMS

First published in 1999 by Sutton Publishing Limited

This new paperback edition first published in 2007 by Sutton Publishing

Reprinted in 2009 by
The History Press
The Mill, Brimscombe Port,
Stroud, Gloucestershire, GL5 2QG
www.thehistorypress.co.uk

British Library Cataloguing in Publication Data
A catalogue record for this book is available from the British Library.

ISBN 978-0-7509-4943-9

Front endpaper: Hagley Street, Halesowen, at the beginning of the century. Most of the Black Country was in Staffordshire, but Halesowen, Cradley, the Lye and Stourbridge were south of the Stour and were therefore in Worcestershire, along with Dudley which was in a detached part of the county. Whatever their ancient history, the thing that Black Country towns had in common was their rapid nineteenth century growth – creating the bustling Edwardian towns seen here and in following views. This postcard was produced by H. Parkes, whose shop is in the centre of the picture. (*Ken Rock Collection*)

Back endpaper: We began our journey through the century and through the Black Country in Halesowen, with a view of a typical Edwardian Black Country High Street. We end our journey back in Halesowen, with another kind of view. The topography of the region provides plenty of interesting vistas – such as this one – where the whole interwoven complexity of Black Country manifests itself: high streets, industry, residential areas, green areas, areas in decline and areas of renewal. (*Dave Whyley Collection*)

Half title page: Maybe Black Country high streets could look like any others, but the coal on which Black Country prosperity was built was never far away. In 1906 some work on a sewer uncovered the coal beneath the main street in Bilston. In 1914 Cradley Heath High Street 'crowned in' as a result of coal mining. (*Ken Rock Collection*)

Title page: Mrs Burgin and her son, Alfred, in the doorway of the family's shop at 167 Wolverhampton Street, Dudley, 1905. Edwardian newsagents' shops – or paper shops as they are called in the Black Country – tended to cover themselves in enamel signs and billboards. (*Don Bytheway Collection*)

Typeset in 11/14pt Photina.
Typesetting and origination by
Sutton Publishing.
Printed and bound in England.

Contents

Metal bashing has always been synonymous with the Black Country – nicely caught in this stylised picture of men at work on the two-ton forge hammer at John Folke's Lye Forge in the 1960s. (*BCS Collection*)

Foreword

THE PRESIDENT OF THE BLACK COUNTRY SOCIETY

As President of the Black Country Society I take considerable pleasure in seeing another book about our region take to the bookshelves. When the Black Country Society was formed in 1967 there were very few books on the subject. The society was founded by enthusiasts who felt that the region had not received fair recognition of its great contribution to the industrial development of Britain and the rest of the world, nor were its unique characteristics being celebrated locally. The Society wished to see the region put back on the map for both those who lived inside and outside it.

The Society's aim was to bring together all those who shared an interest in the past, present and future of the Black Country. The rapid growth of the Society, now with a membership approaching 3,000, and the popularity of its widely acclaimed quarterly magazine, *The Blackcountryman*, and the growth of an increasing number of town and community based societies with similar interests, demonstrates that local people have responded positively to initiatives to keep alive a sense of belonging to the Black Country.

The Society was formed at a time when the local government reorganisations of 1966 and 1974 seemed to threaten the survival of a local sense of identity, and the term 'Black Country' was not being used in a very positive way. Now there are over 100 local firms using the term in their business names, and in 1987 the government gave some official recognition to the use of the term by creating the Black Country Development Corporation. The four metropolitan boroughs created in 1974; Wolverhampton, Walsall, Dudley and Sandwell, now all acknowledge that they administer an area called the Black Country even if its traditional boundaries are not quite the same as their own new boundaries.

A great opportunity was lost when Wolverhampton Polytechnic became a university – it could have become the University of the Black Country. Perhaps we can hope for a Bishop of the Black Country or a Lord Lieutenant of the Black Country in the not too distant future. Perhaps sometime in the next millennium we will become the Green City of the Black Country. Whatever happens, playing with names and agonising about boundaries doesn't seem to matter – our sense of being the Black Country just grows stronger than ever!

As a publisher of many books, as well as *The Blackcountryman*, the Society recognises the importance of books, recorded memories and photographs in preserving our heritage and passing it on to the next generation. Sutton Publishing's sub-series, *The Black Country in Old Photographs*, with some twenty titles and over 50,000 sales in the past five years, has contributed greatly to all this, and the Society welcomes W.H. Smith's decision to become involved in publishing two local pictorial histories to mark the millennium: the other deals with Wolverhampton.

It is a challenge to claim that any book covers the Black Country, even if looking only at this century. Its content has to cover a wide geographical spread, a complex history, and a great diversity of twentieth-century activities. Every Black Country township from Willenhall in the north to Halesowen in the south, from Walsall in the east to Kingswinford in the west will hope to be represented, and we can expect to see every kind of human activity covered from chain-making to carnival queening.

This book charts a century of change in which our region began with a vague sense of being the Black Country and ended with certainty about it – having lost nearly all claim to industrial 'blackness' in the meantime! I commend this book to you. The author is a founder member of the Society, and with his prolific output of books about the area has contributed much to the present positive position.

Tony Copson

These chaps and wenches could be outside any Black Country boozer just before the First World War. Chaps wear caps, waistcoats and mufflers, wenches wear white smocks. A typical Black Country pub has a central entrance between two shallow bay windows, plus an 'entry'. (*Author's Collection*)

Britain: A Century of Change

Children gathered around an early wireless set in the 1920s. The speed and forms of communication were to change dramatically as the century advanced. (*Barnaby's Picture Library*)

The delirious rejoicing at the news of the Relief of Mafeking, during the Boer War in May 1900, is a colourful historical moment. But, in retrospect, the introduction that year of the first motor bus was rather more important, signalling another major adjustment to town life. In the previous 60 years railway stations, post-and-telegraph offices, police and fire stations, gas works and gasometers, new livestock markets and covered markets, schools, churches, football grounds, hospitals and asylums, water pumping stations and sewerage plants had totally altered the urban scene, as the country's population tripled and over 70 per cent were born in or moved to the towns.

When Queen Victoria died in 1901, she was measured for her coffin by her grandson Kaiser Wilhelm, the London prostitutes put on black mourning and the blinds came down in the villas and terraces spreading out from the old town centres. These centres were reachable by train and tram, by the new bicycles and still newer motor cars, con-nected by the new telephone, and lit by gas or even electricity. The shops may have been full of British-made cotton and woollen clothing but the grocers and butchers were selling cheap Danish bacon, Argentinian beef, Australasian mutton, tinned or dried fish and fruit from Canada, California and South Africa. Most of these goods were carried in British-built-and-crewed ships, burning Welsh steam coal.

As the first decade moved on, the Open Spaces Act meant more parks, bowling greens and cricket pitches. The first state pensions came in, together with higher taxation and death duties. These were raised mostly to pay for the new Dreadnought battleships needed to maintain naval superiority over Germany, and deter them from war. But the deterrent did not work. The First World War transformed the place of women, as they took over many men's jobs. Its other legacies were the war memorials which joined the statues of Victorian worthies in main squares round the land. After 1918 death duties bit even harder and a quarter of England changed hands in a few years.

Women working as porters on the Great Western Railway, Paddington, *c.* 1917. (*W.L. Kenning/Adrian Vaughan Collection*)

The multiple shop – the chain store – appeared in the high street: Sainsburys, Maypole, Lipton's, Home & Colonial, the Fifty Shilling Tailor, Burton, Boots, W.H. Smith. The shopper was spoilt for choice, attracted by the brash fascias and advertising hoardings for national brands like Bovril, Pears Soap, and Ovaltine. Many new buildings began to be seen, such as garages, motor showrooms, picture palaces (cinemas), 'palais de dance', and the bow-windowed, pebble-dashed, tile-hung, half-timbered houses that were built as ribbon-development along the roads and new bypasses or on the new estates nudging the green belts.

During the 1920s cars became more reliable and sophisticated as well as commonplace, with developments like the electric self-starter making them easier for women to drive. Who wanted to turn a crank handle in the new short skirt? This was, indeed, the electric age as much as the motor era. Trolley buses, electric trams and trains extended mass transport and electric light replaced gas in the street and the home, which itself was groomed by the vacuum cleaner.

A major jolt to the march onward and upward was administered by the Great Depression of the early 1930s. The older British industries – textiles, shipbuilding, iron, steel, coal – were already under pressure from foreign competition when this worldwide slump arrived, cutting exports by half in two years and producing 3 million unemployed (and still rising) by 1932. Luckily there were new diversions to alleviate the misery. The 'talkies' arrived in the cinemas; more and more radios and gramophones were to be found in people's homes; there were new women's magazines, with fashion, cookery tips and problem pages; football pools; the flying feats of women pilots like Amy Johnson; the Loch Ness Monster; cheap chocolate and the drama of Edward VIII's abdication.

Father and child cycling past Buckingham Palace on VE Day, 8 May 1945. (*Hulton Getty Picture Collection*)

Things were looking up again by 1936 and unemployment was down to 2 million. New light industry was booming in the Home Counties as factories struggled to keep up with the demand for radios, radiograms, cars and electronic goods including the first television sets. The threat from Hitler's Germany meant rearmament, particularly of the airforce, which stimulated aircraft and aero engine firms. If you were lucky and lived in the south, there was good money to be earned. A semi-detached house cost £450, a Morris Cowley £150. People may have smoked like chimneys but life expectancy, since 1918, was up by 15 years while the birth rate had almost halved. The fifty-four hour week was down to forty-eight hours and there were 9 million radio licences by 1939.

In some ways it is the little memories that seem to linger longest from the Second World War: the kerbs painted white to show up in the blackout, the rattle of ack-ack shrapnel on roof tiles, sparrows killed

A family gathered
around their
television set
in the 1950s.
(*Hulton Getty
Picture Collection*)

by bomb blast, painting your legs brown and then adding a black seam
down the back to simulate stockings. The biggest damage, apart from
London, was in the south-west (Plymouth, Bristol) and the Midlands
(Coventry, Birmingham). Postwar reconstruction was rooted in the
Beveridge Report which set out the expectations for the Welfare State.
This, together with the nationalisation of the Bank of England, coal,
gas, electricity and the railways, formed the programme of the Labour
government in 1945. At this time the USA was calling in its debts and
Britain was beggared by the war, yet still administering its Empire.

Times were hard in the late 1940s, with rationing even more stringent
than during the war. Yet this was, as has been said, 'an innocent and
well-behaved era'. The first let-up came in 1951 with the Festival of
Britain and then there was another fillip in 1953 from the Coronation,
which incidentally gave a huge boost to the spread of TV. By 1954 leisure

motoring had been resumed but the Comet – Britain's best hope for taking on the American aviation industry – suffered a series of mysterious crashes. The Suez debacle of 1956 was followed by an acceleration in the withdrawal from Empire, which had begun in 1947 with the Independence of India. Consumerism was truly born with the advent of commercial TV and most homes soon boasted washing machines, fridges, electric irons and fires.

The *Lady Chatterley* obscenity trial in 1960 was something of a straw in the wind for what was to follow in that decade. A collective loss of inhibition seemed to sweep the land, as stately home owners opened up, the Beatles and the Rolling Stones transformed popular music, and retailing, cinema and the theatre were revolutionised. Designers, hairdressers, photographers and models moved into places vacated by an Establishment put to flight by the new breed of satirists spawned by *Beyond the Fringe* and *Private Eye*.

In the 1970s Britain seems to have suffered a prolonged hangover after the excesses of the previous decade. Ulster, inflation and union troubles were not made up for by entry into the EEC, North Sea Oil, Women's Lib or, indeed, Punk Rock. Mrs Thatcher applied the corrective in the 1980s, as the country moved more and more from its old manufacturing base over to providing services, consulting, advertising, and expertise in the 'invisible' market of high finance or in IT. Britain entertained the world with *Cats*, *Phantom of the Opera*, *Four Weddings and a Funeral*, *The Full Monty*, *Mr Bean* and the *Teletubbies*.

The post-1945 townscape has seen changes to match those in the worlds of work, entertainment and politics. In 1956 the Clean Air Act served notice on smogs and pea-souper fogs, smuts and blackened buildings, forcing people to stop burning coal and go over to smokeless sources of heat and energy. In the same decade some of the best urban building took place in the 'new towns' like Basildon, Crawley, Stevenage and Harlow. Elsewhere open warfare was declared on slums and what was labelled inadequate, cramped, back-to-back, two-up, two-down, housing. The new 'machine for living in' was a flat in a high-rise block. The architects and planners who promoted these were in league with the traffic engineers, determined to keep the motor

Carnaby Street in the 1960s. (*Barnaby's Picture Library*)

13

The Millennium Dome at Greenwich, 1999. (*Michael Durnan/Barnaby's Picture Library*)

car moving whatever the price in multi-storey car parks, meters, traffic wardens and ring roads.

The old pollutant, coal smoke, was replaced by petrol and diesel exhaust, and traffic noise. Even in the back garden it was hard to find peace as motor mowers, then leaf blowers and strimmers made themselves heard, and the neighbours let you share their choice of music from their powerful new amplifiers, whether you wanted to or not. Fast food was no longer only a pork pie in a pub or fish-and-chips. There were Indian curry houses, Chinese take-aways and American-style hamburgers, while the drinker could get away from beer in a wine bar. Under the impact of television the big Gaumonts and Odeons closed or were rebuilt as multi-screen cinemas, while the palais de dance gave way to discos and clubs.

From the late 1960s the introduction of listed buildings and conservation areas, together with the growth of preservation societies, put a brake on 'comprehensive redevelopment'. Now the new risk at the end of the 1990s is that town centres may die, as shoppers are attracted to the edge-of-town supermarkets surrounded by parking space, where much more than food and groceries can be bought. The ease of the one-stop shop represents the latest challenge to the good health of our towns. But with care, ingenuity and a determination to keep control of our environment, this challenge can be met.

The Black Country:
An Introduction

Through the medium of photography this book looks at the Black Country in the twentieth century. Our pictorial survey therefore begins at a time when the Black Country had already evolved and had earned this name – a name that some were proud of, and some disliked. Our problem is to mentally travel back to the turn of the century and engage with a story that was already well under way.

The story of an area of Middle England becoming 'black' is a story that begins with the exploitation of the coal that lay abundantly beneath the surface of South Staffordshire. Then comes the business of producing iron, and making things with the iron. The major economic activity of the area becomes 'industry', the population grows, transport infrastructure develops, villages become towns, and small towns become larger towns. Urbanisation brings with it problems of public health, sanitation, and the organisation of satisfactory local government. The coal seams become exhausted, land becomes derelict and abandoned. Iron production declines. New industries in chemicals, power generation, engineering and manufacturing emerge. All that was achieved in the nineteenth century.

Our survey therefore begins with coal and iron, recognising that by the beginning of this century the quest for viable sources of coal was taking pit-owners to areas beyond the boundary faults that had defined the nineteenth century coalfield, and that by the 1900s many Black Country folk earned their living outside the primary sector. We then look at the Black Country towns with their busy high streets, public buildings, their new electric tramways, and the facilities that were developing to relieve folks of their disposable income.

The 1900s were a time of prolific postcard production and the cards were very diverse in their subject matter, giving us a fairly comprehensive portrait of the times. Although pictures were taken of the world of work, few seem to have been taken of the domestic scene – and almost none at all were taken of those barren derelict wastelands between towns simply because they were so unphotogenic. Postcard producers like John Price did not shrink from taking pictures of pits and iron works, but were defeated by the prospect of making postcard views of derelict mounds or 'banks'. Professional photographers recorded public events and guide book scenes – and portraiture of those who could afford it.

A Sense of
Occasion. Even
a steelworks
can celebrate a
coronation. The
entrance to F.H.
Lloyd's Steelworks
in Darlaston on
Queen Elizabeth
II's Coronation
Day: 7.40 a.m.
on 2 June 1953.
(*Dave Whyley
Collection*)

The First World War produced quite a rash of photography: almost every young man had his picture taken in uniform before embarking for the front, and pictures were taken of fund-raising events on the home front and even of the world of work adapting itself to the war effort and the shortage of male labour. The only subject that was hardly photographed for public consumption was war damage itself. When the Zeppelins flew over the Black Country in 1916 very little precise information was released about what had happened in words or pictures.

During the interwar years local newspapers became much more pictorial in their content, and the use of cameras became more widespread. We have a lot more choice of surviving images when it comes to portraying the 1920s and 1930s. And, of course, people who were born in those decades are still around to pass on their photographic archives. (Some, unfortunately, still get passed on to the refuse collector rather than the local historian!)

Interwar photographs show a Black Country that was still very Victorian with Edwardian additions, but which was changing in many fascinating detailed ways: traffic increases in the street scenes, the trams gradually disappear to be replaced with trolleybuses and motor buses, shops and public buildings gradually go 'modern', fashions change and the pursuit of leisure develops new trends. The topography of the Black Country changes with the building of the Birmingham to Wolverhampton New Road, opened in 1927, and towns push outwards

A Sense of Community. A feeling that one belonged to a community could be found in the Black Country in chapels, carnival processions, parties held to celebrate great events, or night after night down the boozer. This book does not feature many scenes of domino matches, whippet racing, darts or pigeon racing, but here's a typical Black Country pub: the Royal Oak in Salop Street in 1965, one of thirteen pubs to be found in the 400 yards between the Old Strugglin' Mon, and the New Strugglin' Mon. (*Dave Whyley Collection*)

into new estates – both municipal and private. Local Government changed with some of the old Urban Districts becoming absorbed by the Boroughs, and in some cases they actually became Boroughs in their own right. (For example, Bilston and Rowley Regis both became boroughs on the same day in 1933.) On the work front coal miners virtually became extinct except in the deep pits. Each Black Country town continued to prosper as a result of the specialisms it had developed within the worlds of metal bashing and engineering.

The Second World War produced its own crop of photographs – of the Home Guard and Air Raid Wardens, of Spitfires bought with locally collected funds, and with industry turning to the war effort. Rarer material like life in an air raid shelter, or interaction with the GIs, may have been photographed more informally and such images appear here only because of the diligence of a collector. Once again the local press was often a little coy about showing too much of what was happening on the home front.

Since the Second World War the use of photography has exploded and somewhere there must be a photograph of everything we could be interested in. Therefore there should be an even greater variety of images in the last three chapters of this book, but it can still be difficult to assemble the images that will portray how things have changed. Sometimes, for example, pictures seem to show how little things changed, and many 1950s photographs show changes of fashions and vehicles while the topographical details have a pre-war look!

The Black Country begins to change dramatically in the 1960s, and the changes themselves begin to wipe out the past, rather than co-exist

A Sense of Cultural Identity. When the Black Country's identity was threatened in the 1960s, its culture was quickly reinvented in the form of 'Black Country Nights Out', books of dialect verse, and a new injection of life into local folklore. Here are the John Franklin Singers at their first concert at Brierley Hill Town Hall in October 1975. John Franklin, and accompanist Marjorie Penn, are seated in the centre – but this is 1975, and by now no show would be complete without an appearance by Dolly Allen! Dolly is on the extreme left of the group and her son Ken is on the right. (*Margaret Woodhall Collection*)

with it. Clean air wiped out the blackness of the Black Country, followed by de-industrialisation and a desire for a greener environment. Local Government changes in 1966 and 1974 almost wiped out our sense of where we lived – inventing new concepts like the West Midlands County and Sandwell. Wolverhampton even seemed to join the Black Country if the signs were to be believed! Ironically the response was to create a new interest in the region's past and its identity. It was in the mid-1960s that the Black Country Society was formed and people spoke of the need for a Black Country Museum.

The 1980s witnessed massive bold attempts to reclaim the Black Country – to clean up the mess created by 200 years of being a sprawling industrial workshop. Central Government, who had always seemed unable to recognise the existence of the Black Country as a distinct and unique social and geographical entity, suddenly decided to use the term Black Country in a decisive moment of direct intervention in the region's affairs – in 1987 the Black Country Development Corporation was created.

The area has tried to regenerate itself and reinvent itself. No more coal working, no more steel making, no more areas of derelict waste on which horses might graze, no more parochial communities – but just fine modern 'integrated' towns and new expressways on which to drive to the multiplexes or the shopping centres! Growth industries have been in the service sector, and the Black Country has awoken to tourism. At the beginning of the twentieth Century it was difficult to find any part of the Black Country that could truly be described as suburban, at the end of the century that is what it is becoming.

The Start of the Century

The 'multiples' arrived in the Black Country in the 1900s, and were soon represented in every town – competing with each other, and local family businesses and the Co-op. Here the staff of the Maypole Dairy Company pose in their hessian aprons outside the shop in Wednesbury. (*Ken Rock Collection*)

Fetching coal and working iron were the two activities which had led to the meteoric development of the Black Country in the nineteenth century. Even at the beginning of the twentieth century, many pits were still small and were worked by teams of subcontractors. This pit on the Earl of Dudley's Himley Coalfield displays fairly modest winding gear, with the old horizontal 'gin' in the background. (*BCS Collection*)

The twentieth century did see coal mining develop on a larger scale. The semi-exhausted small 'gin' pits were replaced with deep mines delving into the thick coal just beyond the faults that plunged the seams to greater depth. Believing that its output would be considerable, the Earl of Dudley founded Baggeridge Colliery as a modern deep pit. Work on the first shaft began in 1899, this photograph was taken *c.* 1910 but it was 1912 before the pit went into full production. (*Ken Rock Collection*)

Several John Price postcards showed scenes at the Earl of Dudley's modern colliery at Baggeridge, and on the other side of the Black Country the pits at Jubilee and Hamstead. To men brought up on the traditions of the small pits the size of the frame and engine house at these pits was most impressive. These men may be visiting the pit, or may be working on lining the shaft, in what appears to be a picture taken at Jubilee which opened in 1910. (*Ken Rock Collection*)

Washing, screening and wagon-loading facilities were laid out at Baggeridge on a scale not seen before in the Black Country. The rail connection was provided by the Earl of Dudley's own railway system and linked the pit to his own steel works at Round Oak, to many wharves from which the coal was sold, and to the GWR at Baggeridge Junction. The pit lasted until 1968. (*Jim Evans Collection*)

Some people define the Black Country by the limits of the South Staffordshire Coalfield; others use the one-time presence of the iron trades as a test of Black Country 'membership'. Up until the 1880s the area produced iron at a number of blast furnaces. This activity then declined except where it was replaced by steel-making. By then many communities had developed specialisms in working the iron into various products as opposed to producing the material itself. Alfred Hickman's works at Spring Vale made the transition from iron-making to steel production and survived until the end of the 1970s. It was much featured in John Price postcards such as this. (*Ken Rock Collection*)

Each Black Country town acquired a reputation for a specialised iron product; casting, moulding, rolling, stamping, forging iron into saleable commodities. For example, here at Swindell's, are the edge tool manufacturers of Netherton – holding examples of their work, *c.* 1910. (*George Edwards Collection*)

Working in iron could entail working on your own at the back of your home or being part of a huge industrial enterprise. The Patent Shaft & Axletree Company at Wednesbury grew out of various Black Country traditions – the local production of iron, followed by local specialisation and inventiveness, and by absorption of smaller businesses. These 1906 pictures show railway equipment being made for export. (*Author's Collection*)

These pictures were taken in the Patent Shaft's Old Park Works. The works spread over a large area and the Patent Shaft managed to survive until 1980. This part of the works was demolished in March 1994. (*Author's Collection*)

23

In the south-west of the Black Country iron was forged into nails and chain – often in small workshops on a 'sweated' basis in which the self-employed worker bought the material, worked it and then sold it back as a finished product to the same middleman. Small firms such as Noah Bloomer in Oak Street, Quarry Bank, developed who were also able to 'prove' or test the chain. Horse-drawn drays provided transport, as can be seen in this Edwardian photograph. (*John James Collection*)

This scene at one of Noah Bloomer's hearths was replicated in many small workshops, many of which were at the back of people's homes. Although machine-made welded chain, and machine-made nails came along, some demand for hand-made chain has continued to this day. (*Rob Day Collection*)

Industrialisation and urbanisation did not create a solidly built-up environment. Remnants of agriculture and vast areas of dereliction still kept each Black Country settlement physically separated from its neighbours. This postcard view from Oldbury, looking towards the Rowley Hills at Rounds Green, taken in about 1910, captures the feel of the local landscape. (*Ken Rock Collection*)

Many Black Country communities remained rather village-like, although they would probably have preferred to be called small towns. They often grew up literally in the shadow of local industry. Albright & Wilson's stack and chemical plant tower over the main street in Langley, *c.* 1910. In Wednesbury, Brierley Hill and Bilston it was a short walk from the High Street to massive steel works. (*Ken Rock Collection*)

Not everyone in the Black Country was bashing metal, nor was there anything unusual about women working in the Black Country. This is a Horace Dudley postcard view of workers at the Manifolda Stationery Company in West Bromwich. (*Ken Rock Collection*)

Local co-operative societies expanded their services as funds permitted. For example, a venture into bread production would later be followed by bread delivery, first from one cart and then with others. In this turn-of-the-century view it can be seen that the Walsall Society is expanding in this way. (*WMCS Collection*)

Palethorpes Ltd provides a good example of the growth of a Black Country business. Henry Palethorpe moved to Dudley in 1873, and his son moved the manufacturing side of the business out to these premises in Tipton in 1890. By the 1900s they were supplying sausages to all parts of the country via the railway system. The factory was an established Black Country institution until its closure in 1966. (*BCS Collection*)

Over the years Palethorpes opened about twenty shops like this impressive one in Birmingham Street, Oldbury. The firm was progressive in marketing its products, using advertising and packaging to good effect. In the late 1980s some work on restoring the commercial life of this part of Oldbury led to the sign on the Simpson Street wall of the shop being repainted, although you can no longer buy a Palethorpes sausage from the shop. (*BCS Collection*)

Transport had played a major role in aiding the development of the Black Country – first the canals and then the railways. This early twentieth-century view of the canal passing through the man-made cutting in the Galton Valley gives the false impression that the canals were not busy. The horse-drawn narrowboat has passed under Telford's graceful road bridge, beyond which is the GWR railway bridge – now the location of a new railway station. (*Ken Rock Collection*)

An Edwardian postcard view of Walsall railway station. The wooden buildings are of the partly prefabricated style found at a number of LNWR stations in the Black Country, while the brick-built buildings on the left date back to the days of the South Staffordshire Railway. The Grand Theatre manages to appear on the skyline behind the 0–6–0 goods engine. (*Ken Rock Collection*)

Electric tramways spread through the Black Country at the turn of the century, sometimes municipally owned and sometimes built and operated by companies like British Electric Traction. Their development produced a conurbation-wide network of public transport that made local people much more committed to road transport than rail for this kind of journey. They also contributed to the growth of suburbia – as in this example of a Walsall tram serving Pleck. (*Ken Rock Collection*)

A single-decker tram from Dudley reaches Five Ways, Cradley Heath on a service that commenced in October 1900. This was the terminus of the line despite the fact that the destination blind reads Cradley. (Extensions were planned to Cradley and Quarry Bank, but never materialised.) The Crown still stands on the left, but the trams ceased running at the end of 1929 and were replaced by Midland Red buses. (*Ken Rock Collection*)

BET/South Staffordshire Tramways car no. 43 on the Dudley–Wednesbury service, seen here at the Tipton Road terminus in Dudley, *c.* 1910. Note the BET 'magnet' trademark on the side of the tram. This service ceased in March 1930. (*Ken Rock Collection*)

Large bogie single-decker trams known as the Cradley Bogies were introduced on the Dudley-based, BET operated, system in 1902. They were soon seen on all the Dudley-based routes and on the light railway out to Kinver. This one advertises Stourbridge Shopping Week in November 1910. (*Ken Rock Collection*)

The tram electrical overhead is brought down through Wordsley High Street on span wires, passing Wordsley Parish Church just to the right of this view. Next door to Wordsley Post Office, on the left, is E.C. Whitney's shop from which he sold ecclesiastical ceremonial garments. The building, with its distinctive dormers, still survives. (*Ken Rock Collection*)

Climbing from the Stour Valley, Stourbridge High Street makes its way into the centre of the town. Some feel that this stronghold of North Worcestershire is not real Black Country, but its industrial history would seem to suggest otherwise. The shops partly obscured by the carriage became the site of the Scala Cinema, opened on 11 October 1920. (*Ken Rock Collection*)

31

In the market-place, Great Bridge, soon after the turn of the century, we find the streets carry tram tracks but little sign of traffic. As in the pictures of Cradley Heath and Stourbridge, there are a fair number of children about – just when did these postcard photographers go about their task? On the left is The Limerick Hotel, on the right is Thomas Turner's coffee house. (*Ken Rock Collection*)

The larger towns could boast civic buildings like Wednesbury Town Hall, seen here on the left. Next door is the Art Gallery, built in 1891 as a bequest to the town by Edwin Richards and his wife. Although giving a certain status to the town of Wednesbury, these buildings had the disadvantage of being rather on the margin of the town centre. The hustle and bustle of town centre activity tended to be found nearer market-places in most towns. (*Ken Rock Collection*)

Another John Price postcard view gives us a picture of Edwardian shops on a grand scale – shops built on two floors and including a pedestrian arcade. This was Bradford Street, Walsall, before the First World War. Wolverhampton had its arcades but only Walsall had shops opening on to a balcony at an upper level. (*Ken Rock Collection*)

Once again we see that mixture of tram tracks, horse-drawn vehicles and emptiness – this time in Smethwick High Street. The trams ran from Birmingham to Dudley through this street as this was the 'old' route between those places before the New Road opened in 1927. The buildings on the right were refurbished by WMCC in the early 1980s, but the left hand side of the street has vanished completely. (*Ken Rock Collection*)

Although postcard views in Edwardian times often show relatively empty streets, many events did fill these streets on occasion: Wednesbury Market Place is well filled for the 1914 Wednesbury & District Co-operative Society Gala – the kind of occasion that demanded that everyone should wear a hat! (*Ken Rock Collection*)

Sunday School Treats and Friendly Society Parades could also fill the streets in the years before the First World War. This one is thought to be a Sunday School procession approaching Christ Church. The Church Tavern, in the background, still exists – having gone through several re-namings. It is currently The Nailmaker. (*Frank Webb Collection*)

Princess Marie Louise of Schleswig-Holstein visited Tipton on 3 August 1909, opened the Nurses' Home in Lower Church Lane, and then proceeded to Victoria Park for a celebration, passing Palethorpes seen in the background of this picture. There has been no shortage of royal visits to the Black Country during the twentieth century. (*Ken Rock Collection*)

In Walsall on 10 May 1910 the Proclamation of King George V was read from The Bridge by the Mayor, who can be seen immediately below the statue of Sister Dora. (*Ken Rock Collection*)

Dudley Castle fêtes were popular events. A pageant of some kind was usually presented in Edwardian times – on the platform by the castle walls. Balloon ascents were also featured on several occasions. This is thought to be July 1905. (*Ken Rock Collection*)

A trip to the country in a horse-drawn brake, or wagonette, was also popular at public holiday times. This convoy is about to leave Carters Green, West Bromwich, in 1914. In the background is the Olympia theatre. Originally opened as the Olympia on August Bank Holiday Monday in 1906, it had always presented film and variety. (*Chris Clegg Collection*)

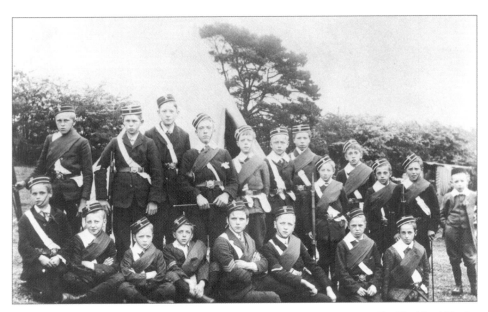

Joining a uniformed youth organisation might produce the opportunity to go to camp. The Wordsley & District Lads Brigade is seen here at Kinver on a Whitsun camping trip in 1909. (*Ken Rock Collection*)

In 1907 a roller skating craze swept Britain and many rinks were hastily provided in urban areas. Large wooden or corrugated-iron sheds were made as commodious as possible, and a rink could enhance its status by providing a band. This is the West Bromwich Rink in 1909. Within a year the craze had waned and the halls were put to other uses. (*Ken Rock Collection*)

Palaces of Variety provided popular theatrical entertainment in the music-hall style. The Empire, Hall Street, Dudley was opened on 3 April 1903 by Dan Leno. (It was built on the site of an earlier wooden circus building.) It later became a cinema on the Gaumont British circuit but succumbed fairly early on – in 1940. In his autobiography Clarkson Rose, the Dudley-born pantomime dame, recalls his youth spent flitting between the Empire and the Opera House. (*Ken Rock Collection*)

Even before 'leisure' was invented, the Black Country working man found time to play or watch football – hence the need to finish work early on a Saturday. In many cases he might play for a Sunday School team or a 'works' team. A team that began life as the Salters' works team had adopted the name 'Albion' by 1886, and two years later Salters' men were playing in the Albion team that won the FA Cup. This picture shows the 1912/13 team. (*Ken Rock Collection*)

The First World War

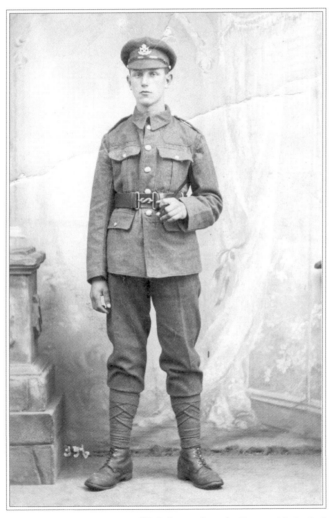

Private William Cox, a Hurst Hill lad about to leave for France with the 2nd Battalion South Staffordshire Regiment. He was spared from doing so as the war ended just as he was about to embark. (*Margaret Woodhall Collection*)

The Kaiser's invasion of Belgium in 1914 created a wave of refugees – some of whom came to the Black Country. Here a group of Belgians line up at the Manor House in Kingswinford. (*Ken Rock Collection*)

A scene on The Bridge at Walsall. The Mayor, beneath the Sister Dora statue which is on the extreme left of the picture, sends off the first recruits from Walsall – with the 5th Battalion South Staffordshire Regiment – on 11 August 1914. (*Ken Rock Collection*)

The Sister Dora statue appears again as Walsall residents gather round the British Red Cross ambulance to which they have subscribed. There were many voluntary fund-raising efforts organised to buy ambulances. One was a scheme to raise £50,000 nationally by collecting all cinema takings on 9 November 1915 to buy a complete convoy of vehicles. (*Ken Rock Collection*)

Pat Collins, the local showman, was a great benefactor of hospitals wherever his fair travelled. He particularly made a point of supporting the Walsall Hospital, and is seen here raffling his horse and trap to raise money to alleviate the deficit faced by the hospital in treating wounded soldiers. (*R. Deeks Collection*)

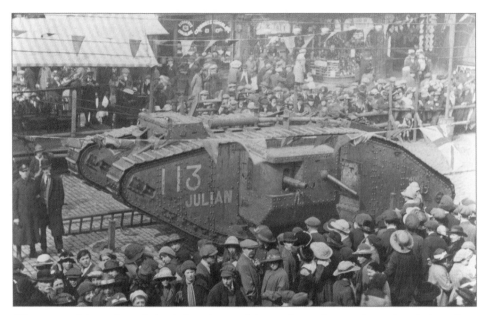

When it seemed that tanks might break the stalemate of the trenches, tanks were also used on the home front to tour urban areas to stimulate saving by investment in Government bonds and saving certificates. Here we see the tank exhibited in Dudley at Easter 1916. (*Ken Rock Collection*)

It seems that the same tank appeared in Walsall's 'Tank Week', and crowds turned out to see the machine parked outside the Town Hall in Lichfield Street. The Mayor, Cllr Slater had to make an official visit, and is probably seen on top of the tank in this picture. (His wife was a victim of the Zeppelin raid of 1916.) (*Ken Rock Collection*)

Fund-raising was also promoted by military band concerts, and this postcard shows a concert in progress in the Market Square at Willenhall in July 1918. At this event it was announced that £204,309 had been raised locally which had paid for eighty-one aircraft. Both the clock tower and Henly's hardware shop are still to be found at the same location. (*Ken Rock Collection*)

On 23 August 1915 Private Arthur Taylor returned briefly to his home, wife and child in West Street, Quarry Bank, while convalescing from the effect of several bad wounds. Here we see bunting and crowds in Bower Lane to greet him. He returned to the 2nd Battalion Worcestershire Regiment and was killed later in the war. (*E. Cox Collection*)

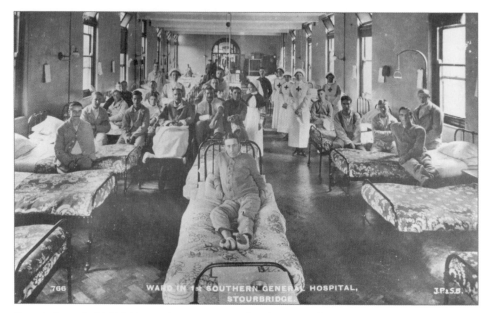

Towards the end of 1916 this was the scene in a ward in the 1st Southern General Hospital at Stourbridge. The temporary military hospital was located in a mansion known as Studley Court. It later became a Catholic girls' school, and was then purchased by Ernest Stevens who presented it to Stourbridge as a Council House. (*Ken Rock Collection*)

Women working for the Midlands Electricity Company in 1917 are seen here laying a mains cable from Ocker Hill to Darlaston via Wednesbury. Some had official studio photographs taken of them in their uniform – just as the men had such a photograph taken before leaving for the front! (*Ken Rock Collection*)

The Zeppelin raids of
31 January 1916
caused loss of life and
damage in the Union
Street area of Tipton
and in Wednesbury. Two
Zeppelins, *L21* and *L19*
of the German Navy,
flew over the Midlands,
possibly hoping to bomb
Liverpool and generally
intimidate the British
civilian population. It
seems that they were
probably lost when
passing over the Black
Country, but their
bombs killed thirty-five
local people, including
the Mayoress of Walsall.
(*BCS Collection*)

There were shortages of food supplies towards the end of the war and Food Committees were formed to oversee control of prices and some measure of rationing. The shortages still managed to cause unrest and Goodwin's store in New Street is seen here after the Quarry Bank food riots. A well-known local figure claims that one of his grandfathers was inside defending his stock, while his other grandfather was throwing stones from the street! (*Marie Billingham Collection*)

Peace celebrations in 1919 often took the form of parades. This horse and decorated dray was taking part in the Willenhall Peace Celebrations of 19 July 1919. (*Author's Collection*)

The Peace Celebrations at Ellowes Hall, the Gornal home of the Gibbons family, took the form of a garden party. The ladies are, left to right, Floss Griffiths, Lucy Hardwick (the cook at Ellowes Hall), unknown, Ellen Horton, Brenda Hughes, Mrs J.W. Cox and unknown. (*Margaret Woodhall Collection*)

46

The Interwar Years

Ted Bennett Snr and Mrs Parkes in the doorway of the Cradley Heath
Branch of the Dudley Co-operative Society, 1920. The war was over,
businesses were optimistic about returning to 'normal' but a short-lived
'boom' was followed by financial crises – the roller-coaster ride of the interwar years was underway. . . . (*Ted Bennett Jnr Collection*)

As the pits were released from Government control unrest followed wage cuts and increased hours. By 1921 coal strikes were a fact of life in the south-western part of the Black Country. In this picture the committee of the Miners' Distress Fund contemplates the distribution of food purchased after a 'benefit' at Old Hill's Grand Theatre. (*George Edwards Collection*)

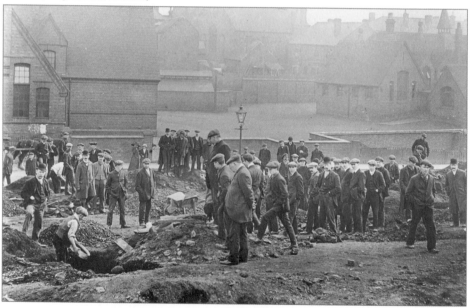

During the 1921 strike out-of-work miners and their families returned to 'coal-picking' on the pit banks as they had done before the war. Many of the small to medium-sized pits between Netherton and Old Hill, and some on the Himley Coalfield were allowed to flood and never reopened. Fetching coal was on the decline in the Black Country except at the deep pits. Scenes like this occurred again in 1926. (*Ken Rock Collection*)

The Black Country was no longer a battle ground with clearly defined territories of Liberalism and Conservatism. The Labour Movement had been gaining ground and nothing could be taken for granted. When Mr Cooper retired from his Walsall Parliamentary seat in 1922 he assumed that the electorate would return his wife in his place. The Liberals selected Pat Collins, the well-known showman, as their candidate, and after a fierce battle he won the seat! (*Author's Collection*)

Parliamentary Borough of Walsall, 1922

MEN and WOMEN of Walsall VOTE for

LADY COOPER, The Unionist Candidate.

POLLING DAY IS

Wednesday, Nov. 15th.

From 8 a.m. 8 p.m

Bilston Municipal Election, Nov. 1st, 1937.
TOWN HALL WARD.

HATTIE HOLLAND

During the interwar years there were many firsts for the Labour Party – their first successful candidates on local Councils, the County Council, and in Parliament. There were also many 'firsts' in all these spheres for women. For example, Hattie Holland was the first and only woman to serve on Bilston Urban District Council (from 1930 to 1933), and was the first woman locally to become a magistrate. (*Judi Hughes Collection*)

49

Scenes in Black Country high streets in the interwar years begin to look different to the scenes portrayed in the first chapter. The electric tramways were gradually abandoned in favour of buses and motor traffic drastically increased – as can be seen in this view of West Bromwich High Street. The presence of new architectural styles slowly made themselves felt in shop fronts, public buildings and cinemas. (*Ken Rock Collection*)

The clock tower at Carters Green marked an important tramway junction where routes from Birmingham divided to proceed to Dudley (74) and Wednesbury (75). On 1 April a 1924 Birmingham Corporation took over the operation of these routes, and one of their cars is seen here passing a West Bromwich Corporation bus in the 1920s. These tram routes survived until 1939. (*Jan Endean Collection*)

Lichfield Street, Walsall, looks very peaceful in this 1920s view of the Library. This postcard view was produced as one of the 'Park Series' of cards for W.H. Smith. (*Ken Rock Collection*)

In the smaller Black Country villages there was a sense, at least visually, that time had stood still, as seen here in Rowley Regis. There might now be one or two visiting motorists replacing those who had once come in pony and trap, but the streetscape still looked as it did at the turn of the century, but for St Giles' Church, occupying a commanding position on top of the ridge. This church had been freshly rebuilt in 1923, after its predecessor, built in 1904, had been destroyed by fire. (*Ken Rock Collection*)

For those municipalities which ran their own public transport, the interwar years were an opportunity for modernisation and expansion. In West Bromwich this Tilling-Stevens TS3 with a locally built Smith body went into service in 1919 with solid tyres and rather pre-war appearance, but by the 1930s West Bromwich had a fleet to be proud of – in a distinctive cream and two shades of blue livery. (*Ken Rock Collection*)

Walsall, like Wolverhampton, wished to display its modern approach to the provision of public transport by replacing trams with trolley buses. This striking six-wheeler in Walsall's blue livery is seen in 1931, about to leave Walsall on the 29 route jointly operated with Wolverhampton Corporation. The new venture into using trolley buses on an 'inter-urban' service began on 13 November. (*Brian Baker Collection*)

With all this motor traffic on the roads, and new innovations like traffic lights, accidents were bound to happen. Here we see the results of a collision at the crossroads by the Fish Inn at Amblecote in the 1930s. The cone of the glassworks behind the Fish Inn was one of many in this area. (*John James Collection*)

Crowds gather in September 1921 to gaze at the results of a runaway on the hill in Perry Park Road, between Old Hill and Blackheath. (Ironically the road had been built to by-pass several with steeper grades!) Burrell road steam locomotive 'Mark Twain', of 1904 vintage, belonging to Pat Collins, has left the road followed by its 'train'. The ornately decorated wagon is the beast wagon belonging to Mrs Collins' Lion Show. (*Harry Mills Collection*)

Building the new Birmingham–Wolverhampton road was a major interwar project. The road stuck to the eastern side of the Black Country ridge and traversed land that was at the time derelict following coal extraction. It crossed numerous local government boundaries, and divided one or two communities in half. It was built by Sir Robert McAlpine & Sons, using steam navvies and contractors' light railways to reshape the landscape. Here we can see work progressing near Bury Hill, Rounds Green, in 1926. (*Author's Collection*)

As the New Road was completed the South Staffordshire Water Company lay new water mains alongside it. Clark Transport is delivering the main between Causeway Green and Jarvis Bridge. After three years' work the road was opened by Edward, Prince of Wales, on 2 November 1927 with eight ribbon-cutting ceremonies – one at each local boundary! (*SSWC/Johan Van Leerzem*)

From the First World War onwards it became more common for women to be allowed to work as 'hands'
behind grocery counters, and deliveries by some shops were motorised. Joe Goodwin's shop, in New Street,
Quarry Bank, was repaired after the riots (see page 45) and between the wars had a large staff. (Joe Goodwin
is second from the left, and his son John Goodwin is fourth from the left). (*Pat Mattocks Collection*)

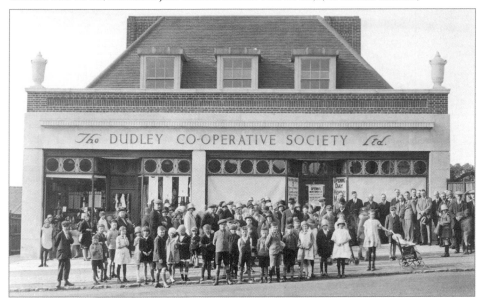

The rival to the private grocer – the Co-op – was also in an expansive mood in the interwar years. On 27
May 1929 we see Dudley Co-operative Society opening its new premises at Pensnett. Crowds had to await the
official opening at 6.00 p.m. (*Ted Bennett Jnr Collection*)

In high streets more modern shop fronts began to make their presence felt by the 1930s. We can see that several stores surrounding Dudley Market Place have adopted new styles, including Peacock's, Universal Stores and Woolworth's. The latter received its new frontage in cream faience tiling in 1930. Trams had ceased running through the market place on 1 March 1930, track was lifted or tarmacked over, but the poles are still evident in this picture. (*Ken Rock Collection*)

Many co-operative societies struggled to build a town-centre department store in the modern style in the 1930s. Dudley's 'emporium' opened on 21 October 1939 – after the war had begun, and had a second 'official' opening on 16 December, which was quite a grand affair. In true-to-form Black Country style construction had been delayed when the builder struck coal while digging the foundations. (*Doris Grubham Collection*)

In the 1930s Castle Hill, Dudley, was transformed into the leisure and entertainment mecca of the Black Country. The Plaza cinema, on the left, was opened on 28 May 1936. Well to the left of this scene Dudley Zoo opened on 5th May 1937. The Odeon, on the right, was opened on 28 July 1937, and the Hippodrome Theatre opened on 21 December 1938. (The last two reappear on page 71.) (*Author's Collection*)

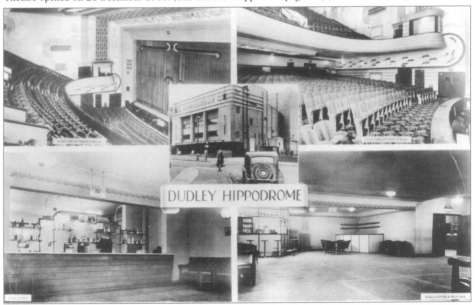

Dudley Hippodrome was a typical 1930s building – and even today the interior has a good art deco-inspired 1930s feel to it, although the building is unlikely to survive far into the next millennium. For almost a quarter of a century it put the Black Country, and Dudley in particular, into the premier league in the world of variety theatre – not realising what a transient world it was. (*Ken Rock Collection*)

How did we look between the wars? Wedding groups sometimes give a good impression of fashion – as in this example where Vera Dunn marries Donald Hill in the summer of 1926. The Hills were jewellers in Brierley Hill, and Donald was among those who defused the incendiary bomb that dropped on Quarry Bank on 19 December 1940. (*Frank Webb Collection*)

Founder members of the Vicar Street Young Men's Bible Class, Dudley – taken in the year it all began, 1927. (*Viv and Brian Turner Collection*)

Doris Downing marries Billy Bennett at St John's Church, Kates Hill, Dudley, 1932. The Downings were a respected brewery and property owning family. (*Viv Turner Collection*)

Now something unusual happens: the photographer, after taking the above picture, turns round and photographs the crowds watching from St John's Street – thus giving us a record of how one dressed for a wedding in 1932, and how one would have dressed if just passing by! (*Viv Turner Collection*)

Ox-roasting was a popular feature of local carnivals, and there was often a charity auction for the first beef sandwich. This picture was taken at the Brierley Hill Carnival of 1927, an event which raised funds for the Burton Road Hospital. (*Ken Rock Collection*)

Part of the ritual of ox-roasting was the business of selecting the 'lucky' victim. At the Darlaston Carnival of 1932 everyone, including the ox, lines up for a photograph. (*Ken Rock Collection*)

The Corbett Hospital fêtes were regular social and fund-raising annual events near Stourbridge. The hospital opened in August 1893 with a grand fête and parade of local Friendly Societies. The building was a gift from John Corbett – the 'Salt King' of Stoke Prior. He also endowed the hospital with a fund, but local fund-raising helped maintain and extend the hospital. This picture was taken in 1927. (*Ken Rock Collection*)

This picture, of 1935 vintage, shows students participating in the annual Dudley Teacher Training College May Festival – better known in later years as 'The Rag'. The college opened in 1907 and in recent years merged with Wolverhampton Polytechnic, the premises thus becoming the Dudley Campus of Wolverhampton University. (*Ken Rock Collection*)

61

Our last look at the outdoor occasions of the interwar years shows the annual 'Hospital Parade' held in Dudley on 10 July 1932. Here the parade marches into the Castle Grounds, led by the Mayor, Cllr Fullwood, passing a banner of the Dudley United Friendly Societies – the umbrella organisation which had organised the event since 1872. (*Ken Rock Collection*)

The same parade is seen gathering in Dudley Market Place. The banner in the mid-distance appears to belong to a Wesleyan Sunday School, but the choirboys in the foreground belong to St Edmund's Church. Over 300 participants from a variety of organisations took part – in warm sunny weather. (*Ken Rock Collection*)

The Second World War

September 1939 – the first month of the Second World War – and children sitting by Rudding Pool in Lightwoods Park, Smethwick, are practising wearing gas masks. (*Smethwick Local History Society Collection*)

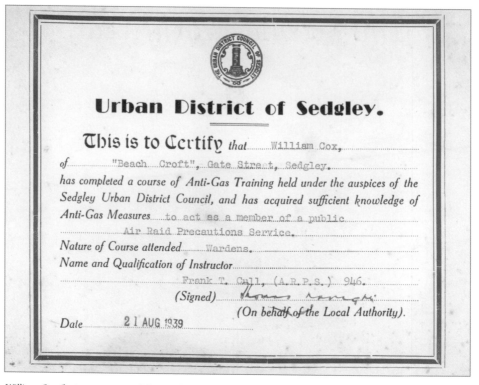

Urban District of Sedgley.

This is to Certify that......William Cox,..

of.........."Beach...Croft",..Gate..Street,..Sedgley............................

has completed a course of *Anti-Gas Training* held under the auspices of the
Sedgley Urban District Council, and has acquired sufficient knowledge of
Anti-Gas Measures.....to..act..as..a..member..of..a..public.........................
................................Air..Raid..Precautions..Service................................

Nature of Course attended..........Wardens.....................................

Name and Qualification of Instructor...
.....................................Frank..T...Call,..(A.R.P.S.)..946..............

(Signed)...........*Thomas...ranaght*......................

(*On behalf of the Local Authority*).

Date...........21 AUG 1939...

William Cox (last seen on page 39) completed his anti-gas training in August 1939, and as soon as war was declared he was able to train the people in his street in the use of gas masks, as a member of the ARP Service. (*Margaret Woodhall Collection*)

At the other end of the war we find William Cox fourth from the left on the front row in Civil Defence uniform. This was the Sedgley Branch of the Staffordshire Civil Defence Corps, demonstrating that there is more than one way to wear a beret, photographed on 8 April 1945. (*Margaret Woodhall Collection*)

Wednesbury Council Gas Team of the ARP Service in the back of a Public Works Department lorry. The team was led by Ray Vaughan, a foreman in the Works Department. Ray's team would disappear for days after the bombing of Birmingham and Coventry on ARP missions, rescuing people trapped in bombed buildings. Many folk worked in some kind of emergency service alongside professionals, and in addition to their 'normal' work. (*Edna Vaughan Collection*)

Another wartime option was to join the Special Constables. This group of 'Specials' came from Quarry Bank. (*Doreen Cartwright Collection*)

65

Most fire brigades had a few full-time staff supplemented by 'retained firemen' who were on call. After the War began these were supported by members of the Auxiliary Fire Service. Practices were also organised with local factory-based fire brigades. Both of these pictures show the Wednesbury Brigade practising with brigades from local firms like Charles Richards and F.H. Lloyd. (*George Reohorn Collection*)

The practices shown here were held by the River Tame at Bescot, just by the railway marshalling yard. Here you can see vehicles produced by Albion, Fordson and Commer. The sign on top of the hut reads: 'Danger – Firing Range In Use'! (*George Reohorn Collection*)

Just as in the First World War, the public were encouraged to buy War Bonds, and engage in fund raising for many causes. These members of the AFS at Oldbury are preparing for some fund-raising with a 'game' in which participants will hurl pennies at Hitler's face – helping to nail him in his coffin. (*Peter Kennedy Collection*)

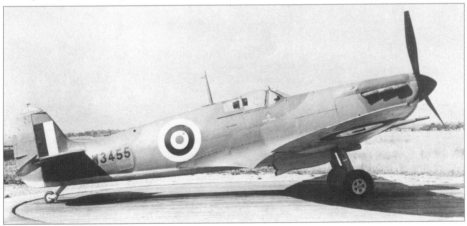

Every town, and many organisations, had a Spitfire Fund. Each fund had to raise a nominal £5,000 towards their Spitfire, and here is W3455 'Smethwick' waiting for the call. Fourteen days after entering service the records simply state 'FTR' ('failed to return'). (*Peter Kennedy Collection*)

'Dad's Army' – the Home Guard at Mitchells & Butlers Brewery at Cape Hill marching through the brewery yard with bayonets fixed. (*Peter Kennedy Collection*)

A house in Hales Lane (now St Marks Road), Smethwick, was destroyed by the crash of a German Heinkel bomber on 10 April 1941. It was shot down by F/Lt Deansley and Sergeant Scott from their 'Defiant' aircraft based at Tern Hill. Five local people were killed, together with two German airmen. Two other German airmen survived. Part of the engine can be seen on the pavement. (*Peter Kennedy Collection*)

An immediate reaction to the declaration of war was to dig trenches and order sandbags. Here the boys of Holly Lodge Grammar School, Smethwick, dig trenches in the autumn of 1939. Pupils from this school were later evacuated to a school in Newport, Shropshire, for a time. (*Peter Kennedy Collection*)

Pictures taken in air raid shelters are very rare indeed, but here we see the Taylor family in their shelter at the corner of Trafalgar Road and Windmill Lane, Smethwick. All generations are represented, and the dog. An extra steel pillar in the foreground adds strength to the roof. (*Peter Kennedy Collection*)

Once again many women found work as a result of the war, and as a result of 'directed labour'. Phyllis Rudd worked in a greengrocer's shop and fancied working on the railway. Driving a horse for the LMS Road Traffic Department wasn't quite what she had in mind. Here she is – with 'Jack' in the LMS yard at Willenhall (Stafford Street). (*Phyllis Rudd Collection*)

Katherine Carrol is seen here on munitions work at Avery's, West Bromwich. She had an artificial arm as a result of a wound when working on munitions at Albright & Wilson during the First World War. (*Peter Kennedy Collection*)

Early in 1945 children are seen queuing outside the Odeon, Dudley, to take part in a 'salvage collecting' competition organised by the manager, Joe Alexander. He was manager at the Odeon from 1944 to 1956. (*Joe Alexander Collection*)

On the opposite side of the road (Castle Hill), on a sunnier day the previous year we find Amy Hill sitting on the Dudley Hippodrome steps. Amy worked in the theatre's box office. The hoarding in the background advertises 'Soldiers in Skirts' – a drag show performed by American servicemen. When first presented at the Hippodrome the Watch Committee decided such material was not suitable for Dudley people and only GIs were allowed to see it. They later relented and the show returned on several occasions. (*Amy Shepherd Collection*)

71

In 1943 a contingent of the 8th US Air Force Signal Corps took over the Worlds Wear factory in Beakes Road, Smethwick. About a hundred 'Yanks' were based there, and many made friends with the locals. US Airman Eddy Allen is seen here with Muriel Payne (left) and her sister in a real period photograph. After the war Muriel travelled to the USA and married Eddy. (*Peter Kennedy Collection*)

Towards the end of 1944 Sergeant John Blasek USAF, stationed at Beakes Road, Smethwick, married local girl Margaret Green. Eddy Allen, on the far left, was his best man. Jo Green and Doreen Willets were bridesmaids. Both the Blaseks and the Allens are still living in the USA today. (*Peter Kennedy Collection*)

The Postwar Years
and into the 1950s

Teddy Gray, rock-maker to the Black Country, poses his new postwar Austin van beneath the keep of Dudley Castle. (*Teddy Gray Collection*)

Amy Davies buys the first motor scooter to take to the roads of Wolverhampton, 1946. The Swallow Gadabout was produced by the Swallow Coachbuilding Company (part of the Helliwell Group) at Walsall Airport. As coachbuilders they had specialised before the war in side-car manufacture. This was a quick return to peacetime activity – using their pre-war skills with engine technology from Villiers. (*Amy Davies Collection*)

Opening on 23 December 1946 and taking us into 1947: the annual pantomime at Dudley Hippodrome was *Jack and the Beanstalk*. Left to right: Mavis White as Princess Dorothy, Beryl Stevens as Jack, George Betton as King Brazenface and Roy Royston as Dame Halleybut. (*Bob Hosier Collection*)

A.E. Chapman & Co. of Old Hill prepare for life to return to normal, having just taken delivery of some new Bush radios. (Television is still on the horizon.) Their van still carries its wartime white paint on the mudguards and there still isn't much to look at in the shop window. Half a century later the firm is still operating from the same premises. (*Mrs Green Collection*)

At this time most domestic heating was still provided by burning coal, some of which still reached the retailer via canal boats. This is the Albion Wharf, West Bromwich, in the late 1940s and R.B. Tudor Ltd have replaced their pre-war horse-drawn drays with modern motor lorries. (The stables in the background, have become a garage.) Two of the boats, the *Stroud* and the *Charity* belong to the firm and bring coal to their wharf from the Cannock pits. Coal production fell during the war, but the company seems to have a healthy stock pile on the right. (*Robert Tudor Collection*)

In the early postwar years many Black Country folk still went hop-picking just as the autumn school term began. Most formed tightly knit groups that returned to the same hop yards year after year. The producers, out on the Worcestershire/Herefordshire border, provided accommodation in 'barracks', as seen at the back of this picture, or barns. These pickers, from the Dudley area, were photographed in 1948. (*Bob Hosier Collection*)

Annie Tibbetts and her daughter Sylvia are photographed by the hop-pickers' crib, *c.* 1950. They travelled to the hop fields as part of a group from Quarry Bank. (*Sylvia Shaw Collection*)

By the 1950s many local bus operators were able to begin replacing their worn-out pre-war fleets. This Leyland Titan PD2/1 with a Park Royal body was supplied to Walsall Corporation in 1951, and is seen here at the St Pauls Street bus station. It carries fleet number 127, and the full width front was perhaps designed to make it conform to the appearance of Walsall's trolley buses. (*R. Hood Collection*)

West Bromwich Corporation also invested in new buses in the postwar era. Fleet number 156 was a Daimler CVG5, and was introduced in 1952. It has just passed the Willie Holt Billiard Hall on the road that now forms part of the Ringway, but was then St Michael's Street. (*R. Hood Collection*)

An August Bank Holiday in the early 1950s brought crowds to Dudley Castle and the Zoo: it may be August but it's best to take a coat! In June 1951 the Castle Grounds had been used to stage a Festival of Britain pageant, but it had rained continuously for ten days. (*Author's Collection*)

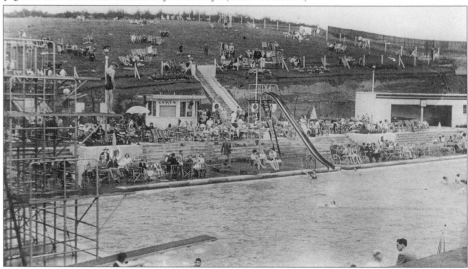

The Wall Heath Lido behind The Kingfisher, therefore also known as The Kingfisher Pool. It opened in 1934 but was at the height of its popularity in the postwar years. It later closed and the buildings have become a Country Club. (*Ken Rock Collection*)

When Queen Elizabeth II's coronation came along in June 1953 it seemed to herald a new age in which the last world war could firmly be put behind us. Many buildings were decorated to mark the event and here we see the Clifton Cinema in Coseley celebrating it. Perhaps cinemas were particularly keen to participate, and to present a film of the occasion, as it was one of the first national events to be presented to the nation via television. (*Sandra Gwilliam Collection*)

A Coronation Party scene – behind a public house in Darlaston, June 1953. (*BCS Collection*)

On 28 July 1954 the Walsall Co-operative Society was able to welcome its 100,000th member. President Tom Gwinnett and Secretary George Taylor make a presentation to Marjorie Garner. The wooden panelling of the board room, then in the Bridge Street premises, is now to be found in the board room of the West Midlands Co-operative Society in Hatherton Street! (*WMCS Collection*)

By 1954 the Dudley Hippodrome was filling many weeks of its schedules with local talent shows. Here we see The Silver Songsters preparing make-up and costumes before going on stage in the 'Pick of the Midlands Show'. The girls were from Celia Couper's dance troupe based in Amblecote. (*Celia Thorneycroft Collection*)

The 'Sausage Room' at Marsh & Baxter's factory in Brierley Hill towards the end of the 1950s. High standards of hygiene and a concern for public health now prevailed. The firm, a major employer in Brierley Hill, is still remembered for one of its advertising images: a pig pulls along a cart of sausages, 'drawing his own conclusions'. (*Phil Millward Collection*)

Working on the thread rolling machine at Nuts & Bolts (Darlaston) Ltd. The Foster Street firm had been established for fifty years, in an industry traditionally associated with Darlaston. (*R. Hood Collection*)

The pantomime at the Dudley Hippodrome running from December 1956 into 1957 was *Dick Whittington*. Here we seen a party of employees' children from Richard Thomas & Baldwin of Brierley Hill on their annual treat. School caps are still worn, but duffle coats are making an appearance. (*Frank Power Collection*)

If a trip to the pantomime was a winter treat for Black Country children, then a trip to Dudley Zoo was a summer treat. The elephant Meena gives children a ride in the 1950s. Holidays abroad and the family car have relegated a trip to the local zoo to being something less of a treat, but the Zoo has survived and found new ways of providing a meaningful experience for visitors. (*Dave Whyley Collection*)

Both pictures on this page were taken towards the end of the 1950s, capturing the essence of a landscape still waiting to change. This residence, presumably a former public house, stands on the Dudley Road at Round Oak – and the steelworks virtually seem to be in the back garden! (*Bill Bawden*)

Looking down the flight of the Delph Locks in the late 1950s as a horse-drawn boat emerges from the penultimate lock. The picture is taken from Ninelocks Bridge in Mill Street, Brierley Hill. (*Bill Bawden*)

Once again we return to Dudley Market Place to get a sense of how things looked at the end of the 1950s. There is still a sense of time standing still: vehicles have changed and a few shop names like Littlewoods and Marks & Spencer have appeared, but it still looks much as it does on page 56! (*Bill Bawden*)

Broadway Hall had been built to accommodate increasing numbers of students coming to Dudley Teacher Training College and it seemed very bright and modern compared to other halls of residence in the late 1950s. A Midland Red D7, of 1955 vintage, negotiates the island on its way back to the bus station from the Priory Estate. (*Bill Bawden*)

The Bostin' '60s and '70s

Lady Jayne & Royaltee: the Black Country's Mamas & Papas with a California sound that came all the way from Tipton and West Bromwich. Lady Jayne was Anna Terrana, whose brother Phil also played in the group. (*Keith Farley Collection*)

Danny Cannon & the Ramrods, from Bilston, seen winning the Big Beat Contest at the Gaumont, Wolverhampton, 1961. Danny Cannon (né Robinson), sporting a gold lamé jacket for the occasion, supported by Len Beddow, Pete Walton, Ken Hooper and Alan Lacey, went on to record as Herbies People and Just William. (*Len Beddow Collection*)

No sixties 'hop' was complete without a Conga! On 5 February 1964 the Conga gets going at the Dudley Guest Hospital Staff Dance at the Station Hotel. (*Viv Turner Collection*)

The 'bricks & mortar' environment may have stood still in the immediate postwar years but by the 1960s things were changing fast, both in the High Street and out on the new housing estates and tower blocks. In this view of Brierley Hill High Street, both the Co-op and Littlewoods are in the new functional style that had been developed as the 1950s progressed, and then appeared everywhere as the 1960s unfolded. (*Bill Bawden*)

New functional styles of building were coupled with other ideas about separating pedestrians from traffic in increasingly congested towns. These ideas led to the building of shopping precincts – and no town was swinging in the '60s without one. The Churchill Precinct in Dudley swept away Victorian Hall Street in a scheme that was started in 1962 and completed in 1969. This picture was taken in 1970. (*Ned Williams*)

By 1969 the Churchill Precinct was completed and Beatties had moved into the section facing a widened King Street. The bridge seen here conveyed shoppers to and from a huge car park carved out of a slum clearance area around Flood Street. Dudley advertised its three attractions as the Zoo, shopping and free parking. The Zoo survived, Beatties survived, but the other shops and the free parking are things of the past. (*Bill Bawden*)

More modest than the town-centre precinct was the suburban shopping piazza. This example, at New Invention, featured double-decker shopping, again presented in brutal 1960s style. (*Ned Williams*)

The shopping piazza at Kingswinford was equally bland around the perimeter but was saved by a wonderful circular dome which became a MEB showroom. (*Bill Bawden*)

The Russells Hall Estate was an experiment in building on derelict land that had been extensively worked for coal. The scheme exploited the 'Dudley Rationalised House' that was built on a concrete raft for stability and was made from prefabricated sections that could be quickly erected on site: 390 houses were completed in ten months in 1965. From the estate there are views of the new tower blocks. (*Bill Bawden*)

The Brierley Hill flats are rising above The Delph in this 1967 view taken from the mound of one of the derelict fireclay pits looking towards Delph Road. In the 1970s some of this derelict land was opencasted and drastically re-landscaped before being built on. (*John James*)

The end of steam: shunters and controllers from the Open Hearth Shop face the withdrawal of steam locomotives on the Round Oak Steel Works private railway system in June 1963. (*Jack Reynolds Collection*)

The end of steam: on Saturday 29 July 1962 the last train ran between Wolverhampton and Stourbridge Junction via Dudley. 'Prairie' tank engine 4173 made the journey in darkness: it was not just the end of steam – the Beeching axe had fallen and the line closed. Other services were dieselised but were withdrawn later in the 1960s. (*Express & Star*)

Young railway enthusiasts interviewed the driver and fireman before making the last trip to Stourbridge Junction on 29 July 1962, perhaps not realising that the withdrawal of this service was only the beginning of three decades of drastically 'rationalising' the Black Country's railway system. (*Express & Star*)

91

The end of steam: a Scammel Showtrac of 1947 vintage tows away one of Pat Collins' steam road locomotives, past the Albion Mill in Walsall. The Foster engine, of 1921 vintage, is on its way from Bloxwich to the Griffin Foundry at Oldbury on 29 August 1963 where it will survive in preservation. Many engines ended their lives in scrapyards. (*Stan Webb*)

On 5 March 1967 the last trolley bus ran from this turning circle in Dudley (Stone Street) to Wolverhampton. No longer would the No. 58 trolley swing round past the Saracen's Head, pause to unload by the newsagents and then take this turn to the waiting shelter. Trolley buses survived in Walsall until October 1970. (*J. Simpson/R. Hood*)

In the mid-1960s West Bromwich Corporation ordered fourteen Daimler Fleetline buses. These rear-engined buses with folding door front entrances seemed very modern and were built to a low body height to enable them to drive beneath the aqueduct at Tipton. They looked smart in an all-over cream livery. No. 105 is seen here passing the Tower cinema, which closed at the end of 1968. In October 1969 the local municipal bus fleets were taken into the West Midlands Passenger Transport Executive. (*R. Hood Collection*)

The West Midlands Constabulary had been formed in 1966, bringing borough police forces together to police the five County Boroughs established by local government reorganisation of that year. Modernisation included the introduction of 'Panda Patrols' equipped with radios. This Panda car is parked outside the Odeon, Dudley, which ceased showing films in February 1975. (*R. Hood Collection*)

Flower-power in Bloxwich. On Saturday 19 June 1965,
Marianne Preece is crowned Bloxwich Carnival Queen
by the members of the folk group The Settlers. What
was it about the '60s? The hair? The clothes and
shoes? The music? The end of steam? The birth of the
shopping precinct? England winning the World Cup?
(*Marianne Roberts Collection*)

Billy Smart's Circus Parade enters the Walsall Arboretum, July 1965. Marianne Preece, Bloxwich Carnival
Queen, waves from the shoulders of the second elephant. In the 1960s you could still dream of riding an
elephant without wondering if it was 'politically incorrect' to do so. Perhaps that is why the world ended in
1969. (*Marianne Roberts Collection*)

The Eve Hill 'battlefield', summer 1968: streets had been cleared of old housing and construction of the Eve Hill flats was underway. Thirty-one years later the flats were demolished and a pile of rubble occupied this spot once more (see page 120). (*Ned Williams*)

Eve Hill, Dudley, autumn 1970. The flats have been completed and the work now continues in clearing Salop Street of its old houses, shops and pubs. Very little remained of the Sir Robert Peel when this picture was taken. Strangely, the British Oak on the opposite corner was not demolished (and still stands today), but every other building was demolished for road widening that never took place. (*Ned Williams*)

By the 1960s local people had realised that they wished to preserve the history and identity of the Black Country. The Black Country Society was formed to bring together everyone concerned about the past, present and future of the region and, separately, steps were taken to establish a Black Country Museum to preserve examples of the fabric of the area that seemed threatened by progress. The Museum opened in April 1976, and the site of the village looked like this. (*Keith Hodgkins*)

In 1974 local government reorganisation created the West Midlands County. The County was supportive of the Museum, although the Black Country formed less than half its area. The question of which Metropolitan Boroughs regarded themselves as 'Black Country' arose. Wolverhampton, which had included Bilston and Wednesfield since 1966, wisely chose to join the club. Thus, in this 1978 view of the Black Country Museum, we find Wolverhampton's Broad Street bridge taking a central place in the rapidly growing museum. (*Keith Hodgkins*)

Modern Times

Within the first year of the 1980s Bilston's Blast Furnace was demolished and at Patent Shaft staff learnt that the works was to close. Round Oak closed in 1982, followed by Richard Thomas & Baldwin's. Everywhere jobs relating to the steel industry were vanishing. On 27 April 1990 the last steel was made at F.H. Lloyd's in Darlaston, and another 180 jobs disappeared. First hand melter Bill Harris shakes hands with Works Director Alan Johnson as the last shift turns its back on the furnace. (*Express & Star*)

Scenes like this at Round Oak Steel Works were about to vanish as the last two decades of the twentieth century got underway. The diesel shunters out-lived the steelworks, and three were eventually put to work at the Round Oak Steel Terminal when that opened in 1986 on part of the old works. (*Dave Whyley*)

Throughout the 1980s the industrial scene was visually dominated by dereliction, abandonment and demolition. Here in July 1989 we see Hingley's great works at Netherton biting the dust – where once the *Titanic*'s anchor had been forged. As in so many locations, new industrial estates have replaced this kind of landscape – but no one has yet made an industrial estate that makes an exciting photograph. (*Ned Williams*)

As steelworks closed, jobs were lost and the Black Country landscape changed. Large works, like F.H.Lloyd's in Darlaston, seen here on 23 July 1985, dominated the scene, even if surrounded by patches of derelict land on which Black Country folk grazed their horses. The last two decades have seen such locations reclaimed and put to new use. (*Ned Williams*)

The collapse of the steel industry had numerous knock-on effects. For example, it had a considerable effect on the world of scrapyards. Black Country steelworks had consumed vast quantities of ferrous scrap and a network of yards kept them fed. There were men as devoted to scrap as there were others devoted to the furnace – one was George Dorset, seen here in his yard at Willenhall in 1989. (*Ned Williams*)

While giants went to the wall, taking many lesser concerns with them, some small specialists, using traditional Black Country skills, survived. Here Albert the die-caster pours molten aluminium into a steel die at Charter Castings in Great Bridge in August 1990. (*Ned Williams*)

While metal production, metal bashing and engineering battled with recession and de-industrialisation, British Waterways carried on manufacturing wooden lock gates at their Bradley Dock works using traditional materials and traditional skills. The workforce diminished and the number of apprentices was reduced to one, but still they turn out lock gates – as seen here in July 1992. (*Ned Williams*)

If you have spent a lifetime filing metal and making locks what do you do in the 1980s? Tom Millington found that you carry on for ever, but instead of working in a factory you work in a museum! Tom, in his immaculate overall and wearing his trade union badge, carries on filing in 1989 at the National Lock Museum, established at Willenhall. (*Ned Williams*)

New uses for old products: Dorothy Hubble uses cask-making skills at Trevis Smith Ltd, of Cradley Heath, in July 1989, but the end product is now sold as a garden plant tub. (*Ned Williams*)

Although unemployment had been rising in the Black Country since the end of the 1960s, the pain seemed most intense during the 1980s. Whatever industry you worked in, it seemed to be rationalising and down-sizing. Then came cuts and restructuring in the commercial and public sectors. On 29 September 1986 the Freightliner Depot at Dudley closed – it had only opened in 1967! Driver Bill Allsworth and Guard Derek Hillman prepare to leave with the last train through to Carlisle. (*Ned Williams*)

On 6 November 1982 the ABC Savoy Cinema closed in Stourbridge, reducing the number of cinemas in the Black Country from five to four. Operators Tom Watkins and Jan Bruton showed the last film: 'Pink Floyd's The Wall' and twelve more people lost their jobs. Here Tommy, with reel, and Manager Tim Williamson are photographed in part of the cinema never seen by the public – the fire escape from the projection room! (*Ned Williams*)

The Government introduced measures like the Community Programme to deal with long-term unemployment, and created the Manpower Services Commission to deal with the worlds of education and training. As for cleaning the place up and regenerating the economy, the Government decided to bypass local authorities, who were supposed to be cutting their spending, and created Development Corporations. Bill Francis (later Sir William Francis) was put in the 'hot seat' at the Black Country Development Corporation in 1987. Outside his HQ (once the HQ of Accles & Pollack), Bill Francis (right) checks the local 'Who's Who' produced by Sam Ichbia (left). (*Ad News Collection*)

BCDC took on the huge task of decontaminating and stabilising land that had been mined and poisoned for over 100 years. On several sites this was done by removing existing coal, by open-casting the whole area and rebuilding the landscape afterwards. In July 1989 the public were invited on to the Patent Shaft site at Wednesbury to see progress. Deep in this vast hole in the ground old shafts and tunnels were briefly exposed, and were duly photographed. (*Ned Williams*)

After cleaning up the environment, BCDC's main regeneration strategy was to build a new road infrastructure that would open up the area for which it was responsible. BCDC showed little interest in public transport and its faith was put in the building of the Black Country Spine Road. Here we see the road descending from Swan Village to Great Bridge. Already it is surrounded by new buildings – creating the new Black Country landscape. The gas holder was demolished on 5 September 1999. (*Ned Williams*)

Even the Spine Road defeated BCDC, and was only 'completed' by abandoning its planned route and using the section of the A41 seen here between Moxley and Wednesbury. The A41 was widened to cope with Spine Road traffic which now leaves the 'Brave New World' of the BCDC's Automotive Parts Park and makes its way past good local 'old-timers' like Newman Tipper Tubes (left). (*Ad News Collection*)

A retailing revolution began in the mid-1980s, and some shopping traditions have survived, while others have vanished. The concept of the town centre pedestrian arcade was developed in Edwardian times – and has been borrowed and reincarnated in modern shopping complexes, but traditionalists should head for Dudley's Fountain Arcade or this example in Walsall, photographed in 1987. (*Ned Williams*)

Until 1987 it was still possible to go into Harry Cooper's Menswear shop in Willenhall and find Steven Banks using an overhead cash carrier. Made by the Dart Cash Carrier Company of Stoke on Trent, such items are a major element of people's nostalgia for old-time shopping. An example from the Co-op at Lower Gornal was donated to the Black Country Museum: let's hope it sees service in the next Millennium. (*Ned Williams*)

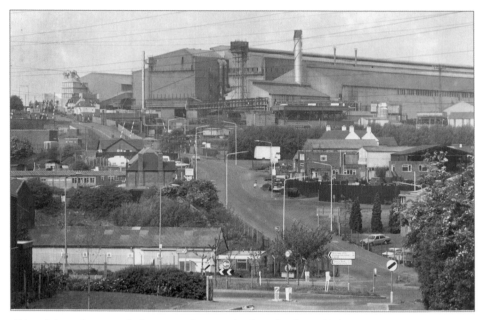

Although it was known in the late 1970s that Round Oak Steelworks would close, the end did not come until 1982. It was therefore possible, at the beginning of the 1980s, to stand in Hurst Lane and look across the Pedmore road to Level Street making its way up to Brierley Hill, with the works still dominating the scene. Now the skyline is dominated by the Waterfront complex. (*Dave Whyley*)

From Pedmore Road it was possible to look back across Farmer Thomas' fields towards the New Level Rolling Mills and Round Oak on the skyline. This is the landscape transformed by building the Merry Hill Centre – replacing heavy industry with retailing and services. (*Dave Whyley*)

The Carrefour supermarket was one of the first tenants of this first phase of the Merry Hill development – seen here in the autumn of 1987. Already such a picture is history as tenants change and aisles are completely refurbished. (*Ned Williams*)

The AMC (Now UCI) ten-screen cinema opened on 14 October 1988 at Merry Hill – the first 'multiplex' in the Black Country. This view of the entrance and paybox was taken on the first day but, again, this has now changed and has been glazed to protect customers from the elements. The cinema may move as a result of current plans to enlarge Merry Hill. (*Ned Williams*)

107

The development of the Merry Hill Centre included building a monorail from the Centre up to the Waterfront. The Swiss-built system reputedly cost £21m and took three years to construct. It was opened in June 1991 but has spent more of its life closed than open. Road access to Merry Hill has been slowly improved but public transport access is still limited to buses. (*Ned Williams*)

Many ventures at Merry Hill have come and gone. For two years local showmen opened a funfair for a few days on one of Merry Hill's car parks. It was an attractive fair with many state-of-the-art attractions and a few traditional ones, but the experiment was not continued. This was the scene in July 1992. (*Ned Williams*)

Bus deregulation of 1986 had quite an effect on the Black Country. The new bus station at Dudley has seen a number of operators come and go since then. In this July 1992 picture we see vehicles of three operators – Midland Red West, Stevensons, and Metrowest posing with the castle in the background. A West Midlands Travel bus hides on the left. There are no buses carrying those fleet names in the Black Country today! (*Ned Williams*)

The quest for better public transport has led operators to explore ways of making buses more friendly towards the environment and towards potential passengers. There have been experiments with bus lanes, kneeling buses for easier access, limited stop services and express services, through ticketing and travel card facilities and so on. Here we see a gas-powered bus introduced on the Walsall–Wolverhampton route in 1998, passing the Dale at Willenhall (compare with page 52). (*Ned Williams*)

On 24 September 1995 the Jewellery Line was opened, reinstating a railway line that had been abandoned and providing access from the Black Country to the rebuilt station at Birmingham Snow Hill. The first train halts at the brand-new station at The Hawthorns and the Deputy Prime Minister, John Prescott, pauses to have his picture taken by the engine – loaned by the Severn Valley Railway. The Midland Metro now travels in the space behind the station. (*Ned Williams*)

The opening of the Jewellery Line on 24 September 1995 also saw this new station at Galton Bridge brought into use – facilitating transfer from the Stour Valley line below to this line (see page 28.) The 1990s have seen some remarkable restoration of passenger rail services as well as the building of the Metro. (*Ned Williams*)

What will happen next? Steam locomotives have been seen operating 'specials' on Britain's privatised railway system – even under the wires. Standing on the new bridge built to carry the Black Country Route over the canal and railway line in 1997, it was possible to see the first steam train to make its way along the main Stour Valley line for thirty years. The perfect picture required a canal boat to be passing in the other direction. (*Ned Williams*)

On 30 August 1992 diesel locomotive 31014 was christened 'The Blackcountryman' at a railway open day at Bescot. Left to right, Mr McDowell of British Rail, Tommy Mundon of the Black Country, and Tom Brown of the Black Country Society. The event was organised to celebrate the Society's twenty-fifth birthday and the locomotive is named after the region's number one quarterly magazine. (*Ned Williams*)

Standing in Halford's Lane in May 1997 it was possible to gaze down at the site of Handsworth Junction: the ex-GWR line from Stourbridge Junction is seen coming in on the left. On the right is the former trackbed of the GWR mainline to Wolverhampton, upon which the construction of the Midland Metro is progressing. The land in the centre of the picture once contained buildings associated with Sandwell Colliery. (*Ned Williams*)

On 21 May 1997 a contractor's train is seen moving ballast wagons along the freshly laid track of the Midland Metro through what was once the site of Bilston Central station, which last saw trains in 1972. No sign of the station survives. (*Ned Williams*)

The West Midlands Passenger Transport Executive, created in 1969, became Centro in 1986 and provides infrastructure such as bus stations, while not actually operating the buses themselves. Bilston bus station, photographed in July 1996, close to the retail market and the heart of Bilston, is an example of its work, and now acts an interchange point between bus services and the Metro. (*Ned Williams*)

Midland Metro car No. 6 races past Swan Village on 31 May 1999 – the first day of public service. The line runs from Birmingham Snow Hill through its own very green corridor in the Black Country to Wolverhampton. Having been in the planning, and then construction, stages for so long everyone now waits with baited breath to see if such projects will expand in the next century or will it be a one-off? (*Ned Williams*)

The West Midlands Fire Service was created in 1974 – replacing smaller local brigades. This picture was taken at Willenhall Fire Station in Clark's Lane in March 1991. Left to right: Station Officer Paul Gaymer, Firefighters Graham Samson, Shaun Reynolds, Leading Firefighter Mick Jones, and Firefighter Paul Butler. (*Ned Williams*)

On 21 May 1991 the County Air Ambulance entered service, and is now often seen above the Black Country. It is funded by public donations, and flies from RAF Cosford. The service covers an area much larger than the Black Country, has already added a second helicopter, and is about to add a third, covering an even greater area. (*County Air Ambulance*)

At your service. Many local businesses have been absorbed by larger firms but Firkins Bakery is still a West Bromwich-based company with a smart fleet of shops throughout the Black Country. Donna Evans, manageress, is assisted by Margot Griffiths and Norma Sutton in the Quarry Bank branch in 1998. (*Ned Williams*)

At your service. Markets have struggled to survive in the 1980s and '90s but what Black Country town would be complete without one? Here in Willenhall in the 1980s the market builds up around the town clock and surrounding pedestrianised streets. The clock was restored in order to be able to celebrate its 100th birthday in 1992. (*Jane Wellsbury*)

Circuses still visit the Black Country at several locations. Here we see Sir Robert Fossett's Circus built up on Dudley Zoo car park in May 1992 with two artics drawn up to form an arched entrance to the Big Top. Traditional circus parades have not been seen in the Black Country since the end of the 1960s. (*Ned Williams*)

Travelling funfairs still open in all parts of the Black Country, sometimes accompanying local carnivals, sometimes occupying the dates of the traditional 'wake' of each community. The Pat Collins firm is particularly associated with the area and here we see the Pat Collins fair at Rowley Regis in May 1996. This is always a colourful well-laid-out fair in a pleasant setting. (*Ned Williams*)

In recent times many local carnivals have struggled to survive. Lye Carnival has persisted, and even hosts the only surviving regular street fair in the Black Country – perhaps now threatened by new one-way road systems! On 17 August 1997 we see Lye Carnival Queens taking part in a charity auction conducted in the street. (*Ned Williams*)

The search for support and sponsorship of community activities like carnivals has led in strange directions. Tipton Carnival received help from Tipton City Challenge in the 1990s. Bilston Carnival, seen here, received support from the local college. The Black Country Rock & Roll Club are seen dismounting from their float in Hickman Park, Bilston, in June 1998. Even if the carnival spirit is flagging at the end of the twentieth century, Rock & Roll lives on! (*Ned Williams*)

Black Country folk now fight for a green environment. Local residents living around Priory Park, Dudley, succeeded in saving a few trees in November 1991. Left to right, Chris, Viv and Brian Turner, Pauline Laight, Dolly, Claire and Mick Hollis. (*Viv Turner Collection*)

The Black Country is now a multi-cultural melting pot. If you were a Black Country Buddhist, where would you go in June 1999 to celebrate the festival of Wesak? To the temple in Brierley Hill, of course. Where once the Anglicans and the Non-conformists competed for the souls of men and women, now there are representatives of every faith and of none. (*Ned Williams*)

Preserving the Past. The Black Country Museum was conceived in the 1960s but it is in the last two decades that it has made the most spectacular progress. Up until now adult visitors have been able to say 'We can remember things being like that.' But what will visitors say in the next century? Two Black Country wenches help re-create a past they never knew in this 1999 photograph. (*Ned Williams*)

Preserving the Past. In the last two decades each Black Country Borough has created proper public archives to fulfil a statutory requirement regarding the keeping of records and to facilitate the study of local history. Walsall Local History Centre led the way and Richard Bond, then the archivist, is seen surrounded by Stuart Williams, Joyce Hammond, Chris Latimer, Betty Fox and Ros Brown. (*Wolverhampton Ad News Collection*)

119

The New Black Country. Two-car garages and executive suburban residences built around landscaped pools now stand where coal and fireclay have been removed on a massive scale. Even the railway embankment has been relocated a few times! A class 37 locomotive makes for Stourbridge Junction as it passes Withymoor Village in a green Black Country landscape. (*Paul Dorney*)

The end of the Eve Hill flats: on Sunday 18 July 1999 two of the three tower blocks at Eve Hill, Dudley, were demolished in controlled explosions just after noon – watched by huge crowds. These flats were built in the 1960s and could be seen from miles away. Demolishing water coolers, steel works, blocks of flats and so on is part of the endless process through which the Black Country landscape changes. In the last Millennium it changed more in the last two centuries than in the rest put together. What next? (*Ned Williams*)

Acknowledgements and Picture Credits

Over the years a number of people have generously made photographs available to me. Some of these people have passed away, but I know they provided photographs in the hope that they would be shared with others via eventual publication. Others have helped provide pictures with this particular publication in mind, and have responded to many requests for help at very short notice.

Pictures have been credited to their source. This is not the same thing as saying that the pictures were actually taken by that person – they are simply prints in that person's collection. In this situation every effort is made to fairly acknowledge the use of each photograph and respect people's proprietorial rights. The photographs can be family 'snaps', official photographs taken by institutions, press pictures and the work of commercial photographers. Some photographs, particularly in the first half of the book, have been issued as postcards, and I thank Ken Rock for generously making his postcard collection available. The Black Country Society assembled a photographic collection over the years, but recently handed it over to the Black Country Museum for safe keeping: I thank both organisations for making this collection accessible again.

Jan Endean of the Wolverhampton firm Eardley-Lewis has worked hard, and at great speed, in preparing prints for publication.

Many people contribute to a publication such as this, and inevitably someone will be left out, but I wish to thank the following – arranged in alphabetical order:

Joe Alexander, Kathleen Bailey, Brian Baker, Mike Ball, Bill Bawden, the Black Country Museum (in particular Louise Tromans), Ted Bennett, Marie Billingham, Mary Bodfish, T. Burford, Donald Bytheway, Doreen Cartwright, Chris Clegg, the County Air Ambulance, Rob Day, R. Deeks, Paul Dorney, George Edwards, Jim Evans, the *Express & Star*, Keith Farley, Teddy Gray, Doris Grubham, Sandra Gwilliam, Stan Hill, Keith Hodgkins, R. Hood, Bob Hosier, John Hughes, John James, Peter Kennedy, Johan van Leerzem, Pat Mattocks, Harry Mills, Philip Millward, Frank Power, George Reohorn, Jack Reynolds, Ken Rock, Patrick and Sylvia Shaw, Amy Shepherd, Smethwick Local History Society, Kathleen Thompson, Celia Thorneycroft, Robert Tudor, Viv and Brian Turner, Frank Webb, the West Midlands Co-operative Society, Margaret Woodhall, Dave Whyley, *Wolverhampton Ad News*.

The information in the captions could not have been compiled without the help and resources now available at the Archives and Local Studies Departments of each of the four Black Country boroughs.